HOW IT WILL
BE FROM
NOW
ON OUT

How It Will Be from Now on Out

poems

Marte Carlock-Clifford

COPYRIGHT © 2023 MARTE CARLOCK-CLIFFORD
All rights reserved.

HOW IT WILL BE FROM NOW ON OUT
Poems

ISBN   978-1-5445-3901-0   *Paperback*
           978-1-5445-3902-7   *Ebook*

*For all my sons
with particular thanks to Hal—
son, colleague, editor.*

Contents

WINTER

How It Will Be from Now on Out   3
In December, Early   5
Tracking   6
Nearing Solstice   7
Moons   8
Midwinter   9
Powder Day   10
Cross-Country on the Golf Course   11
After the Storm   13
Snow, Dancing   14
Skeleton Trees   14
Skiing above Vance Cabin   15
On Buttermilk Mountain Lift   16
Wildcat Mountain, Morning   17
Lunch at Ullrhof   18
Haiku for Dogs   19
February Near Boston   19
If I   20
Fragments from Anywhere   21
Earth Colorless   22
Evening, February   23

SPRING

Wachusett, March   27
6 A.m., April   28

Voice in the Night   29
Sagacity   29
Haiku after Winter   30
Canoe on the Assabet   31
On Gates Mountain   32
Cathedral Spruce Trail   33
AM-FM Stereo   34
On the Ethics of Killing a Stinkbug   35
Painting the Window Sill   36
Bug on the Bathroom Floor   37
Mount Adams   38
Orbiter   39
Demoting Pluto   40
Crocus   41
Visitors   42
Battle   43
Roadkill   43
Town Green   44
Seedling   46
Lucky I Was   47
Baby Picture   49
Refuge   50

SUMMER

Morning, before Commencement   53
Gemini   54
Birthmonth   55
Fog   56
Seeing   57
At Cold River   58
Peril   59

Fireflies 60

New Deck 61

Cycling on Route 30 62

Haiku for Black-Fly Season 63

Haiku, Calm Morning 63

Stung 64

Bass 65

Purple Loosestrife 66

Haiku for a July Dusk 67

Naumkeg 68

Summer, After Sunset 69

Mid-June, 42° North 70

Atop Tyringham Cobble 71

Fireworks as Metaphor 72

Desert Astronomy 73

Haiku for Owl's Head Trail 74

On Mount Adams 75

The Ridge 76

Leonids 77

While Pulling Ivy off Tree Trunks 79

Cycles 80

Journeys 81

Light in Twilight 82

Journey to the Berkshires 83

August Storm 84

AUTUMN

Marked 87

Feather 88

Wings 89

Invasive Species 90

Hillside   91
Haiku for a Hot September   92
Haiku for October   92
Canada Geese   93
In Front of the Bagel Shop   94
Elegy   95
Aspen, Autumn   96
Behind Window Drapes   97
Summits   98
October   99
You Will Know   100
After A.E. Housman   101
Beech   102
Another Pronged Moon   103
Squashes   104
Twigs   105
Crop   106
On Reading Billy Collins   107
For Granted   108
Inspired by e.e. cummings   109
Inspired II   109
Another Country   110

About The Author   113
Credits   113

Winter

HOW IT WILL BE FROM NOW ON OUT

Close to nadir
    when treeshadows reach out to clutch the north
    the sun relents
    lets the earth taste sugar season

dissolves winter's stone into chardonnay
    discloses greens, bristles, garlands
    a week ago imprisoned for all time

On treetops of iron and zinc
    vacuumed clean by November
    an electricity crackles
    from twig to twig

In optics I catch one electron
    sleek sunbreasted
    masked neat as a domino
    cedar waxwing glances at me
        eyes aspark
        and turns again to dine
        on barberry, dogwood, rose hip

They show me berries
    in trees I thought bore none
in an hour they are gone
    as if you snapped a switch

...

Tomorrow it will snow

This is how it will be from now on out
    little winters
        interspersed with little springs.

IN DECEMBER, EARLY

On equine legs the runner
    moves into the morning

his lungs tossing up clouds of silver incense
    like a prayer

beyond his blue hocks the fairway
    is steeled with frost

a brass pond
    unfrozen
dull molasses
    mirrors nothing

above the sun
    squadrons of geese
        configured like supersonic craft
    curve their ailerons downward
        settling

TRACKING

Beneath its surcoat of snow
earth is treacherous today
    I am on guard

Ice shatters light above me

Calligraphies are written underfoot
    a man dragging his heels walked this way then back

Coyote crossed, hunting, her prints aligned
    she must have come before the mouse
    drew a little contrail with its tail

Footprints landing far apart would be
    a runner disdaining ice

These pocks and freckles spat
    by power lines and the tips of twigs

I can't say much about the trees, the sun
but I can tell you who has come and gone.

NEARING SOLSTICE

The sun marches down December
    picking a path through bereft woods
until it rises at the farthest corner of the sky

There's a clapboard barn on the Post Road

sidling nearer to it every day
    even the sun I think
        would like to go inside
and winter there.

moons

The sun swallows another remnant moon
and spits the rind out the other side not caring
it ate a fragment of what remains to me

Still I glory in every morning
salute every new moon and
persuade myself it is good to see
yet one more solstice.

MIDWINTER

We sink into the dark season knowing
    it isn't our proper habitat
uneasy, we bring our errands, our candles
    string lights in trees
light the lights of small purposes

like Druids we cut greens
    recite old stories, sing ancient songs, feast
    despair of night's endlessness
we fatten

grudgingly the sun returns to us
light begins to climb the evening

still strung
as the planet leans to sun
    meaning sapped from them
our colored bulbs grow pale, powerless
    a little foolish.

POWDER DAY

Mine are the only tracks
    before me the course falls away
    like clouds beneath an aviator

    its surface ghostly
        insubstantial
    in the scudding air

Repoussed oldgold willows
    form the far frame

in the woods conifers
    have gathered up the powder
        like so much laundry
    leaving the trail too rocky to ski

Climbing I halt to memorize
    brushstroke of branch and twig
oak leaf snipped from tan construction paper

I am a wizard. I touch
    burdened trees with my wand
    they spring up and fling magic at the sky
    I taste crystal

Now I break loose and float
    down after astounding down.

CROSS-COUNTRY ON THE GOLF COURSE

No cloud
    no wind
        nickel moon
            paler than cloud
        rising

under my boots a foot of
    day-old snow
rail tracks cut
        neat
        smooth
    by someone else
        slick going despite the warmth

tomorrow grass will show
    snow will turn to crème brulee
        crusty on top
        sand beneath

today just sun
        silence
        perfection

Impatient with ease I leave the track
    flounder into drifts
    cut trails into the woods

                              ...

        I don't remember why
                except
I've never gone
        that way before.

AFTER THE STORM

In clear twilight after the storm
        three deer cross the stream
to browse in my wetland

how wrong that I stand
on the firelit side of this window
        while they, so beautiful
scrape for their supper in the blue snow.

SNOW, DANCING

Not falling but dancing
    the tiniest of snowflakes freckle the air
        there is no wind
the sun climbs out of the pit of winter
    but offers no heat
    each flake lingers on the frozen ground
and takes its time to disappear.

SKELETON TREES

How do they do it, the trees
    enduring the killing cold
        standing up in their skeletons
            as if to deceive winter
while in their clandestine cellars
    they gather supplies, munitions, allies
and scheme to emerge triumphant
        when it's time.

SKIING ABOVE VANCE CABIN

Dappled with flecks of spruce
    like an Appaloosa horse
the great white ridge
    swayed boneback spine of the continent
                rises
    against blinding sky

laboriously we mount
    riders of the mountain
        stand inhaling space and distances
then on the wings of Pegasus
                soar.

ON BUTTERMILK MOUNTAIN LIFT

Suspended between heaven and earth
    in a bubble of wellbeing

I read the calligraphy of snow
        stroke of ski
            glyph and chop of rabbit and vole

through nylon and polypro
    sun blesses my knees
        my forearms
I could sleep

below
            snowboards pass
            with a sound like surf.

WILDCAT MOUNTAIN, MORNING

Where the lift chair
           crosses Catamount Trail
    snow guns
         throw up argent atmospheres
         quartzcrystal confetti
            incense rising to meet sunfall
               starclouds
                   sunshot

out of golden mists they come
    wraithlike
        shadows
        then flesh
flocks of skiers
            like angels descending

LUNCH AT ULLRHOF

Darwin was right
    evolution sometimes goes too far

our feet are unfit
we clamber about
    like seals on land
clubfooted
    jerky
        haughty

puffins
    colored like macaws
    plumed in hot lime and plum
    mango and peachglow
we strut and feed

Then still crippled on the snow
    struggle to the place of incantation
with Merlin's gesture fit our stumps with wings
    wizards entering the element of birds
            we fly

HAIKU FOR DOGS

Woods edge, a pocket
    of sun. Across frozen grass
the dogs run, happy.

FEBRUARY NEAR BOSTON

Boring and incessant,
titmouse declares it's spring
he said the same thing in December

What a liar.

IF I

If I had my way we
would tear out the walls of the house
let the sun march in and ruin the furniture
never close a drape
lie amid the roaring of the stars and never sleep.

FRAGMENTS FROM ANYWHERE

    Tamarack knits ochre lace
        prints it on the pond
            gold on coffee
like a greeting card
                on the ridge the trees are stripped to comb teeth

Crow sits on a stumpstub
    looks both ways
        hops down and
crosses the road.

EARTH COLORLESS

Earth colorless waits
    abandoned by winter
    untouched by spring

I wait
    mistrustful

I know spring for a thief
    a mountebank
        he juggles his dazzling gifts
            sun
              pollen
              juices
    we gawk
        mesmerized
                while

with his other hand
    he picks our pockets

a year each time

when we were young
    we welcomed spring
    not thinking what it cost

    I know the price now
it's not a bargain I meant to make

EVENING, FEBRUARY

The sky ripens like a peach

I meant to meditate but cannot bear
    not to watch

tufts of snow are caught
      in clumps of thorn

today I heard the titmouse shout his name

Five weeks shy of equinox
      the earth balances itself
         like a diver visualizing his descent

           ready not ready to plunge

Winter still unfinished
    a spring poem springs up

Spring

WACHUSETT, MARCH

Mothholed ice
    crumbles like a cracker
    walking
        there's nothing you can trust

at the junction
    new signs
        stout and clear
        boulder-buttressed
unite High Meadow and Jack Frost trails

I sit and eat

Breath of breeze
    chills my pack-wet back
chickadee flirts
pileated paroxysm erupts
            then it is silent
        sun strong on my face
        I lean against the signpost

satisfaction:

    spring snow
    dry rock
    knowing where I am.

6 A.M., APRIL

Expecting another April-gray day
    I open the curtain to see my window filled
        with paradise as imagined by Christians
        spread gold-red across the sky

even as I watch the glory bleeds out
    to lemonade
    to bleach-blank
    to monochrome
    to gray

a nanosecond
a glimpse
    and gone

beauty is like that
love is like that
life is like that

VOICE IN THE NIGHT

Somewhere in the forest
    at the fulcrum between sundown and dawn
now and then an owl speaks
      just one syllable
in a voice almost like mine.

SAGACITY

How does the owl come by his reputation for sagacity?
I'll tell you how
    he sits on a branch and listens
like a judge in court

no flitting around like a flycatcher
      if he leaves his branch it's for love or dinner
he doesn't say much
    now and then he asks a question
but he hears everything
      everything.

HAIKU AFTER WINTER

Cardinal today
proclaimed his kingdom. I hope
it includes my yard.

CANOE ON THE ASSABET

Whoever called a river emerald green
    failed to see

    this one is old brown velvet
        like seats in an antique opera house
maples rise ridged and many-trunked
    piers of a great nave

    every twig bears a warbler

the river is obsidian
on its night
    galaxies of pollen
        shift
        mingle
        orbit

ON GATES MOUNTAIN

From steeplebush five yards from my boots
    flight erupts
    beats ponderously four times
    then sits on the wind
        circling
        eyeing me

No need for binoculars
I turn with her
admire her feathers layered like scales

The man who owns this hill comes here on wheels
    pushing cacophony before him
    has never seen the eagle

Suddenly there are two
    her mate gyres
    stops deadstill above me
        icepick beak hooked against the sky

I feel like prey
put a dense pine at my back and watch
        menaced and blessed.

CATHEDRAL SPRUCE TRAIL

But for one
    the giants are gone
    their gothic beams fallen

the last one gangles
tufted at the top
          like a bottle brush
    eighty feet tall
          a hundred years old

Under elbows of deciduous trees
    spruce progeny
        no taller than I
jostle and crowd
extend their branches tentatively
    into the space where the trail
        smooth as city pavement
        tunnels through them

Like a politician campaigning
I gently press their fingertips
        as I pass.

AM-FM STEREO

Rude bleeps and burps of static
spoil the credo
still it is a marvel
    to travel encased in music

In his lifetime
        princes were not so privileged

landscape lit by summer morning
    moves past at speed unimaginable
    two days' journey in an hour

    and his players, his chorus, go with us
    like some celestial visitation

Haydn
    hurtling with me through Vermont
    would have owned it a miracle.

ON THE ETHICS OF KILLING A STINKBUG

Harmless insect
    the Audubon lady says
    just looking for a warm place
to winter. Mary Oliver
    would gently pick it up and take it out the door
    would find a rare philosophy
    beneath its scabrous carapace
But I abhor crawly things
    where there is one there will be many more
        it is a war
        we can't cohabit this, my space
I will kill it, collect
    it in a Kleenex and
    accept the karmic destiny.

PAINTING THE WINDOW SILL

As I was painting the window sill
    a mosquito lit in the wet paint
        there was no saving her even if I wanted to
    she had no way of knowing how or why
        that place once safe had changed

I guess the cosmos works like that
    where sometimes for reasons unexplained
rash decisions yield happy consequences
        and routine ones are fatal.

BUG ON THE BATHROOM FLOOR

The size of this comma, so small it has no identity
no head or tail or limbs that I can see
although it moves in one direction, so it must know

In a so small a creature is there room for brain?
it travels without purpose right left north south
circling doubling back, can't make up its pinpoint mind
stops as if to contemplate, moves across the wide blue tile
paces as if trapped, recoils at grout

Not a likely meal for some larger entity
not even big enough to be a nuisance
I should capture it, see if it would magnify
into something I might recognize
but I can't pick it up; paper edge is insurmountable

Or I could destroy it, as yesterday
I stepped on its twin, so little substance
I couldn't feel its corpse beneath my toe

Now here it is again, aimless, useless
I start to feel akin to that. Suddenly
    as if it hears a silent order
it crosses grout without a pause
marches to the baseboard
        disappears

I hope I get a message like that today
what to do, where to go.

MOUNT ADAMS

How like a public figure
    from afar it seems perfection
        cleancut of profile
        upright
        aloof

closer up it's chaos
    huge blocks of matter
    from an uncivil age
        accumulated in no particular order
            unassimilated

Proof writ again in rock
    that charisma is accidental
    and not at all reliable.

ORBITER

Below Casseopia
    it rises from the trees
    a planet in the north
        an inhabited star

    swift
    relentless
slices the sky and vanishes

For those who ride it
    the sun sets sixteen times a day.

DEMOTING PLUTO

What did he expect anyway
>he never played nicely with the other planets
>went his own peculiar way wandering off for no reason
until finally we noticed he was just too different.

Nobody thinks of him anymore
>just an idea out on the fringe of everything.

CROCUS

    Stubborn
you never learn

April and April you spend
    your bloom on hostile days
        cringing from sleet
        huddled in snow
        closed for self-protection half your life

couldn't you wait a month
    until flower is in style

No

    heedless
    impatient
        you spread imprudent petals
in happy
    self-satisfied rebellion.

VISITORS

When the snow is finally gone
in the garden I find those small plastic species stakes
> scattered
Panola, Viola, Primula, Dianthus

calling cards from last summer
not saying whether they will return.

BATTLE

The bird wakes me up
        slashing at the slider door glass
        a metaphor for us all
fighting with himself

Every time he attacks he shits
        evidence of his anger

                another metaphor for the senselessness of war.

ROADKILL

It should be easy to kill a crow with an automobile
He assesses your approach with a calculating eye
takes one more peck at his meal
at the moment of impact hops to safety
    insolent
like an adolescent jaywalking

It should be easy
I haven't done it yet.

TOWN GREEN

East end pegged down by a
                cobblestone
                squat
                clocked
                cockcrowned church
the grass slopes gently down
    a Swiss valley in small
it was a swamp once

I've lived in this town
    longer than any other place
I sit in the easy air
    watching rude children
           kick a ball upslope
the girl as skilled as the boy
    though not as strong

my biking jacket matches
           forsythia blooms
    the maples shed crimson buds
    the pears bear bridal white
        in the grass
           violets miscegenate

I want to write down a poem
but have no pen
there is plenty of paper
though
among the weeds.

SEEDLING

Somehow
    she stepped into the pot
        of her own volition
let him pack earth around her knees

took root
      leafed out
      perhaps will grow into an exotic plant
      an orchid
      a daisy
            poison ivy
At any rate
    she cannot be transplanted
        now.

LUCKY I WAS

Lucky I was a perennial
    not knowing any better
        I dug in my root
    where I fell

the spot looked reasonable enough
        at the time
partial shade
some stone some clay some sand
average nutriments
not too sour or too lime
water enough, almost

Too late it was clear
I grew in a pathway,
    had to withstand
passersby trampling green shoots

    Rodents nibbled
    deer browsed
the gardener pruned my branches
    for his own convenience

Resolute
    I've put out enough leaf
        to stay alive
    saved some stubborn buds for spring

                ...

This season
    maybe
there'll be bloom and fruit.

BABY PICTURE

On the porch swing
    you hold your baby son on your lap

it is a sweet moment
    here is a human being, new
a miracle

yours to teach

    you will teach him to eat, to walk
you will teach him to read
    to ski, to flyfish

so much to learn

He will teach you
    who he is

REFUGE

Cardinal's notes like hammer strokes
    nail down the morning

Barefoot, I run up the driveway
to find the morning paper
    among daffodils

last night the comet hung
    dusty and glorious
      north of here
by leafout it will be gone

nothing lasts
certainty is unknown
coherence unclear
love hard to give

Refuge is in words
in comets and in birds

Summer

MORNING, BEFORE COMMENCEMENT

Ten flights up in Baker Tower
    you can stand inside the clock
    inside its blurred blank light

four great moon circles
        their stiff numerals
        tine-marks on a pie edge

you cannot see the hands

Below on grass three thousand chairs
    green for you blue for us
    cornrowed in perfect order
        await endings
            beginnings

Tomorrow they will be gone
    three trampled aisles the trace of all our feet
        and grass growing back
        silent as the clock

Ten flights up in Baker Tower
    you cannot tell the time

still the hands move
the bells chime

GEMINI

I was born in this green month
    in the heart of my doublestar sign
    the sun swung to the top of the sky

do not know whether I first breathed
the air of day or night
    it was hot as the prairie is hot
    a place hostile
        at least for me

I should have been born here
          under skyless green
I crush a leaf and breathe it in
    breathe sweetfern and cool air
    shadbush and forests.

BIRTHMONTH

Wild berrybush blooming
        punctuates the month's green
    with small bursts of promise

I never much liked green
    never liked my name
        even less this month

a promiser
    whose blossoms set
        such sorry fruit
        scanty
        birdstolen
        bugeaten

the crop always
            disappointment

This year after fifty Junes
    the sky shines cooler
        June's green softer

I've quit looking for pears on the berrybush
Its blossoms asterisk another decade
        promising enough

FOG

Fog is a discipline
        teaching
regard for what is at hand
    not letting us look
        far forward
or often back

strange how we struggle
we'd rather accept dark-blindness
    than this bright limitation
        there is light in its unshaped mass
    we insist we should see

but coolly it closes down

    giving us one thing at a time
    this nun buoy
    this ghosting boat
    this riprap
    that torn tree

focusing
        on this place
            this time.

SEEING

White perfumes of almost-summer
    sweetpepper bush
    whatcolor sweet fern
    wild rose petal pure but golden-hearted
    candelabra of black locust

Maybe at least he can smell them
    the jogger orange-vested
    who runs head down
    deaf and blind
    with audio-clamped ears

when long blue evenings say infinity.

AT COLD RIVER

Birdmusic
                bugsong
The river plays contiunuo
The fish are silent

Birdwarning
                bugwhine
The river sings tenor
The fish listen

Birdtalk
                bugscream
Fish silent as a thought
quicker than flight

Birddescant
                bugmusic
The river plays continuo
The fish are quick
                and silent

PERIL

Dowager hen turkey paces onto the lawn,
    turns and snips a triangle of leaf from the trillium

Chick follows, only one
Lucky we don't have cats I think
    but as the thought lingers a silent shadow
      snatches the chick skyward screaming
Hen squawks once and lifts her wings but knows it's hopeless
    shakes her feathers
      turns and snips leaf again like a Buddhist monk, accepting

There will be other eggs, other chicks.

FIREFLIES

In the duskalmostdark at the very edge
    of vision there's a microflash
I'm not sure I saw it
    maybe a trick of optics
but there it is again single double

Now and then I pick one out against the twilight
    just another beetle flying
    until he signals

The same brilliance as the firefly but not questing
    thinking he's setting a better example
Jupiter hangs high in the south
    a sham, with his steady borrowed brilliance
while the beetle makes his own.

What does it cost the firefly
    that tiny burst of ego
I suppose it's worth it if there's an answer
    from low in the periwinkle.

NEW DECK

Carpenters' marks
    penciled Xs still mar the studs
                the planks
    lumber company stamps
        cryptic green ink and black
    nail head
            punctuating

Yesterday we were prisoners behind glass
today we walk out
            sit among leaves
my son and I lie on yellow wood
        share binoculars
in sky pinched between house and trees
planets reveal themselves
we see the colors of stars
    and satellites
             ghostly
            silent
cruising the headlands of space.

CYCLING ON ROUTE 30

Lordly on my steed
I ride among my people
    graciously greet them all
    linesman jogger officer of the law

Tall swift and serene
    my head armorcrowned
    my eyes secret
I pass among more lowly folk

On the high road death howls past my elbow
    dragons, their breath fuliginous

I am immortal
I ride on.

HAIKU FOR BLACK-FLY SEASON

I wave and swat but
they are infinite, seeking
the pools of my eyes.

HAIKU. CALM MORNING

At my feet the lake
murmurs. A lone kayaker
passes without sound.

STUNG

Schweitzer was aghast
It was my mosquito he said
        but his visitor had killed it
Schweitzer with his reverence for life
        all life
        would have preferred to be stung
although the mosquito possessed the power
        to kill him, Schweitzer
would risk his own existence
        to remain more moral than a mosquito.

It doesn't stop me but I
        never kill a gnat
without thinking of Schweitzer.

BASS

The fly looks delicious
her pursed lips inhale it

it won't go down
such pain

she has lost volition
tries to turn and swim
is tugged to the air
    shudders at his rude touch

hangs stiff knowing herself
    dead

Nice bass says the fisherman
he slips the pain from her throat

I don't eat 'em

tosses her to the river
stunned, she swims into the murk
for a long time she dares not eat

then she forgets.

PURPLE LOOSESTRIFE

One sudden summer
    it was just
        there
paintbox stuff
        puddling at the highway margins
        in river muck.

It doesn't belong
        so they said
    threatens
    must be got rid of
        they said

Still it is a feast
        goes into that category of nature
            with hawks
            orcas
            avalanches
                    destructive
                but worth having.

HAIKU FOR A JULY DUSK

Sun's gone, but its glow
rebounds from a peach-pink cloud
blooming in the east.

NAUMKEG

Stolen from the other end of the world
    the gong stands on the brick terrace
    wanting to be rung.

The guide offers a mallet
    my stroke sounds over the valley
    makes the cows lift their heads
    tombstones in the graveyard tremble
        marble blocks let go and tumble down the mountainside.

SUMMER. AFTER SUNSET

Some nights
        some twilights

when the sky comes down from Canada
the air is too beautiful
               eggblue
                     peachblue
          champagne
flecked with petals and tendrils
        lagoon water
           sandtan
               tangerine
       lemonade
               daylily petal

in the east the moon's a bent dime
        the sky carbon

at any moment
        this eggshell sky is bound to break
    and hatch us fragile
        into worlds we never dreamed of.

MID-JUNE, 42° NORTH

No cathedral feels as holy
    as this evening
I go outside to sit and worship

the topmost twigs are calm
    as a yogi's breath
the world meditates

in the green below is a tawny shape
    that doesn't belong
        she raises her head
I ask her
    did you know your head is too small for your body
we stare at each other

    Eat the weeds from the path, I advise

Carolina wren considers the silence an invitation
a chipmunk answers trying to sound like a bird

the doe turns and picks her way to the bridge
    even on the planks her hooves make no sound.

ATOP TYRINGHAM COBBLE

We are never prepared for such silence
    so near the village

We look down on it like gods

Whitelacecapped steeple
    prim but
        knowing it is handsome
    preens
among ordinary houses

Now and then a vehicle
    voiceless as a fish in a tank
    moves on the road beyond the trees

If you go to the edge
    you can almost hear the brook
        talking to itself.

FIREWORKS AS METAPHOR

Climbing out of a column of fire
    budding blossoming bursting
    color upon color, spray after spray
glory rising out of the dark
    exploding expanding commanding

        dwindling

ended so soon, so soon
leaving no trace on the quiet sky
leaving the silence
        the dark
    the memory of stars showering down.

DESERT ASTRONOMY

That night the sky
    descended crystalline and pure

    to ease our craning necks
    we lay on warm adobe earth
        stubble grass scratching our shirts

She refused to come out
    scorpions she said
    snakes, tarantulas

On colored earth
        echoing the heat of day
my son and I scoped the sky
    swam among the Pleiads
    saw the moons of Jupiter.

HAIKU FOR OWL'S HEAD TRAIL

On the steepest part
I rest. A fritillary
lights on my shin, drinks.

ON MOUNT ADAMS

The glacier must have tired here
      and set its thunderous load down in a pile
          without thinking

in millennia
      no rock has crumbled
      no soil formed
nothing but lichen grows

A thousand feet below me
      the hut
          a microchip
pins sunlight to the col

I descend into the mountain's shadow
I have chosen the wrong trail
          the steep one
I pray.

THE RIDGE

    Where the highway slices through
        the mountain bleeds blue ice

    I lived atop it once. It's
        a ridge not a mountain really
    but on clear mornings I could see
        the far corner of the state and watch
    the city in the valley fill with smog.

LEONIDS

Overhead
        is a blackboard erased many times
constellations hang there
        schematics of their better selves
     like stars projected on the shell of a planetarium
        before the house lights go down

In the thirty-third year of the Leonids
    we were promised a firestorm
           (maybe)
    forty meteors a second
           (maybe)
if it is clear
if earth at the right hour
    rolls into a river of
        celestial grit and gravel
    that will glory and die in our air.

I was born in the thirty-third year of the century
    (not a good Leonid year)

in the sixty-sixth year of the century
    I never thought of stars
in the next great Leonid year I will be ninety-nine

                                            …

carpe noctum
I stand on the deck in wool and down
    crane at the gray flannelsuit sky
        dead as a blind man's eye

constellations hang there
    silent
    grim
    unmoved
Leo rises empty.

WHILE PULLING IVY OFF TREE TRUNKS

I sympathize with your urge to
    climb to the sun
to take advantage of every tendril-hold you touch

I would do the same but
    no good tree has offered me a twig
        as yet.

CYCLES

Day moon to day moon
Neap tide to neap tide
Ochre leaf to green to ochre leaf
Newspaper to fishwrap to newspaper
Tree to fire to ash
Meal to meal
Quarrel to quarrel
Church peal to church peal
Deadline to deadline
Waiting time to thing awaited to waiting time
Promise made to promise kept
    or not kept
        to promise made
Heartbeat to heartbeat
We go on
on
on

on.

JOURNEYS

Our journeys intersected here
       yours whimsical, I thought
            meadow to meadow
            gust to gust
            flower to flower
    mine purposeful, I thought
        up the Interstate
            odometer reeling off
            a mile per minute

    I had a map, a known destination
       why did you
       come this way
           a likelier meadow alluring
           a wind that sent you winging
           an intuited route inherited
                from centuries when no road was here

Our worlds intersect
I see you, windlifted, too late
       we collide with a click
           your juiceless body
       sweeps over my roof and down
       reduced to powder instantly
           by other purposeful vehicles

I'll complete my journey purposefully
       your death before my eyes.

LIGHT IN TWILIGHT

If I were a worshipper
    not knowing what it is
I would worship it, this calm majestic presence
    processing across the nearnight sky like a king
then like a chimera vanishing
I know why, still I am in awe
    knowing it has entered the earth's shadow
    where it has its own night, its own day
moving relentlessly on to meet the sun
    somewhere over Asia.

JOURNEY TO THE BERKSHIRES

All afternoon
    cirrus has set a crystal
        north and west of the sun
            analyzing its spectrum

now rolling along the ridge
    spotlight sun
    stabs my retina

to make it set
    I descend from the height of land
down to the bosom hills
        baby-butt hills
           cat-haunch hills
      bear rug hills
        comforting welcoming hills
    inviting me to sleep.

AUGUST STORM

In a temper the wind
    snatches up armfuls of rain
    flings it past the window
    like sheets being shaken out to dry
like banners brandished by rioting revolutionaries

Furious at having to carry this storm here from the Bahamas
    somewhere in the house it slams a door.

Autumn

MARKED

In a windstorm if it came down its crown would hit the roof
    slice into the attic
    cleave the walls
The arborist pins a tiny orange square to its bark
    the mark of death

Foresters say trees talk to one another
    warn of predators, of infestations, erect defenses

There's no defense against this
Does it know it is doomed? Does the forest know
    now
        or not until the chain saw hits heartwood
Then does the tree's scream throb down its delicate intertwined radices
    reaching through the earth for its companions' fingers
will they miss it?
will they know?

FEATHER

A bird feather lies on the trail
    what a wonder it is
how does it know to begin with
whether to stay tiny and soft
    or become powerful enough
to lift a raptor to the hunt

    With all the colors there are
how does it know which ones to pick
to mark it for its kind
    how can its producer use it for a season
then drop it on the path
worn out as far as the bird is concerned.

WINGS

When I had wings
I refused to fly voiceless
    like the catbird on her silent errands

or the cock who exults only
    when perched on the dung heap

    Flying tore triumph from me
I was dove wings murmuring,
    a hawk rising and keening
or a goldfinch who syncopates
        wingbeat, song
        wingbeat, song
        wingbeat, song.

INVASIVE SPECIES

Benign vine, bittersweet
    lays its tendril fingers on the nearest tree
Oak thinks it doesn't care
O give it time. The tree will find itself re-formed
    fighting for space and air
        into an obelisk of leaf
    ripe to fall in winterstorm
Dead, but not the vine. With no remorse
    for what it's done it wanders off to find more sun.

HILLSIDE

A glacier died here
leaving its enormous organs
erratic hearts and livers
    and

the bones of old trees.

HAIKU FOR A HOT SEPTEMBER

Emulate the wasp.
She doesn't pause to plan or
ask why. She just stings.

HAIKU FOR OCTOBER

The gold is what an
    aging year remits for light
bought from shrinking days.

CANADA GEESE

Listen—my mother would whisper
    the wild geese—

we children ran out into the dusk
    expecting bird silhouettes across the moon
    never saw them, almost couldn't hear
    the high fading conversations
    from wanderers she longed to copy

now they are too many, and lazy
    don't bother to migrate any more

they stay here in serene flotillas
swim idle arcs in scraps of open water
stand one-legged on the ice

still conversing, gossiping

forgetting the coordinates
for flight to Mexico.

IN FRONT OF THE BAGEL SHOP

On wire chairs at a little table
    in front of the bagel shop
I see them every day
    baggyjeaned, sweatshirted
    sharing an illegal cigarette
        mumbling, chuckling
      yelping now and then

Four times their age I am always
    invisible to them
    and they to me, yet
suddenly today I see how like we are
    on the margins of life
    voices cracking
    bodies changing in ways we
        hadn't imagined

uncertain what
    in the end
        we will look like
who we will be.

ELEGY

Never lay me in a casket
my ruined body on display

Lay me in the fire like any used-up thing

Mulch laurel with the ashes
Look at the sun
        think of me there.

ASPEN, AUTUMN

Contemplate a poem like a leaf
yellow, heart-shaped, slick
I picked it up in disbelief
of autumn and finality

Leaf and summer fade. And so does love.

I kept it in a book somehow, somewhere
I sometimes find it, wonder at the then, the now

Today my son picks up its twin
holds it out to me
not knowing it's a talisman

It twists and dances in the air
displays its real identity

It is the ace of spades. I let it fall
It never was a valentine at all.

BEHIND WINDOW DRAPES

The sun she says
    is bad for pictures
        raises the woodgrain on furniture
            fades rugs

she shuts it out
    rejects its light
        its warmth
to keep things exactly
        as they are

shuts out the world too
    altogether a hostile place
    full of unknowns
        and unpredictables.

summits

On the high horizon chunks of sky are set between spruce
like gemstone in a Navajo belt buckle
a sign the summit is not far off.

The way grows steep
crossed with rock slides, mud, an oak fallen across the trail
    ticks and poison ivy
a vandal has smashed a bottle on the ledge

We struggle up
eager to see the land beyond
and stand to look

It is a false summit
the true one lies ahead somewhere.

Walk on.

OCTOBER

Silverplumed seeds rise on the wind
        practice acrobatics in the restless air

        without notice plunge to their fate in the grass

I capture one
        punch it into soil with my thumb
        if it grows I may find out what it is
or I may forget I ever did it.

YOU WILL KNOW

When I stop planting bulbs you will know,
    you will know I don't believe in spring anymore.

For now, I dig the hole
    drop in the promise.

AFTER A.E. HOUSMAN

Half a century and a score
        already gone. Will there be more?
I walk the woodlands in the cold
        to see the maples clad in gold
Crimson bird and sunflame tree
        enough, if this is all there be.

BEECH

Not white and gold like the czarina's palace
    not thundering chorus and dazzling light

The color of heaven is this

    beech grove on Wachusett's slope
        under scrimmed October sun
    glowing

The color of heaven is
    soft evening
    near sundown
    light not falling from the sky
        but rising from the earth.

ANOTHER PRONGED MOON

Another pronged moon
        scythes twigtips in the west
another twilight
another season
        trees naked
the cycles spin so fast

once ponderous as millstones grinding
    now dervishes
    roulette wheels
    tornados
bent on casting us off into the universe

I put away trowel, shears
        string lights
        cut wood
            wait for snow.

SQUASHES

What is it about squashes
    the colors of October land
    greenstriped and cream, tan

and the pregnant orange pumpkins
      massed
      stacked
      piled
    against the side of the barn

what is so satisfying
    even before we carve their smiles
    that we smile to see them

        rotund and proud
        shouting across the cold air
        boasting
            good harvest!
            good harvest!

TWIGS

I hope no neighbor sees me
gleaning twigs like some peasant crone
what I gather will be kindling instead
    of chemical from a store

When I was small we had a gas fireplace
    its ersatz logs stacked one two three
    little blue flames came out of rows of holes
a child's concept of a hearth

my parents knew my brother and I loved it
yet they only lit it on Christmas

too expensive wasteful ran up the gas bill

I swore I'd have a real fireplace in my house, so I do
my grandsons split logs for me, happy in their manliness
my woods rain firewood, their gift to me. I accept it
lay the twigs criss-cross in the hearth so the flame can breathe

fire rises, so old, so bright, so new,
we forget the labor.

CROP

When all my leaves are gone
    my winged seeds breezeblown
       rooted and
         blooming someplace else

beneath my skeleton
    on malachite grass
I'll leave a quilt of gold

      or maybe brass.

ON READING BILLY COLLINS

Yes but Billy I saw same as you
    mullions making a Hopper painting on the wall
    wine and sun turning an enamel tabletop to stained glass

the ordinary day passing unremarked
    so valuable all the same

The difference is you sit smug at your window
    with your sharp pencil and your notebook that can become a bird
    knowing your thoughts will end in my hand
their verticals and serifs ordered
    like a row of carrot tops in the garden

You will never read mine
    which lie dogeared on my desk, tea-stained
a grocery list written on the back.

FOR GRANTED

I take for granted the great globular blooms of rhododendron
        the color of twilight
    anticlimactic after the excesses of tulips and azaleas
for granted the stars of dogwood
    competing with their own foliage
even the happy dandelions so perfectly designed for their lives

I take for granted the sparrows and crows

but never for granted the wind
        coming from who knows where
blowing aside the gnats
    smelling of the sea
    smelling of deserts and open uplands
    smelling green

never for granted you
or the fact that we love each other.

INSPIRED BY e.e. cummings.

Thank you god for this amazing day
for sky-scouring wind
        for hawks' do-si-do
        even the vulture

for rotting ice
    the calligraphy of vole runs

    for snow-spawned water
        running
        running
under our bootsoles.

INSPIRED II

I thank you goddess for this amazingmost day
for dayset moon and dawncall crow
    for shreds of solstice dawn

for This and Is.

ANOTHER COUNTRY

Old age is another country
    a tyranny of sorts
Its citizens don't get to vote
but are compelled to serve the whims
of an erratic despot
Immigrants arrive unwillingly
emigration is not allowed

I didn't expect to be so soon on this train
traveling there express

ABOUT THE AUTHOR

Marte Carlock-Clifford is the author of *A Guide to Public Art in Greater Boston*. After almost twenty years of writing for *The Boston Globe*, she decided it's more fun to make things up. She has published articles, short stories and poems in more than fifty publications. She lives near Boston. This is her first collection of poetry.

CREDITS

Certain poems in this collection were originally published in *Apricity, Avalon Literary Review, Brickplight, Dash, Door Is a Jar Magazine, El Portal, Inscape, Moon City Review, Penumbra, Pudding Magazine, Rosebud, Slab, Steam Ticket* and *Visitant*.

www.ingramcontent.com/pod-product-compliance
Lightning Source LLC
Chambersburg PA
CBHW060532080526
44586CB00012B/705